focus on

NEW
ENGLAND

❖ *inspiring places, beautiful spaces* ❖

This is a Parragon Publishing Book
First published in 2006

Parragon Publishing
Queen Street House
4 Queen Street
Bath, BA1 1HE, U.K.

Produced by AA Publishing

For details of photograph copyrights see page 96
Text © Automobile Association Developments Limited 2006

ISBN-13: 978-1-4054-8752-8

Color reproduction by Modern Age.
Printed in China by CT Printing Ltd.

PICTURES FROM TOP TO BOTTOM:
The tall white tower of Trinity Church has watched over
Newport Harbor in Rhode Island since 1726.

The lion and the unicorn flanking the Old State House in
Boston, built in 1713, hark back to British days.

The Fruitlands Museums in Harvard Village were among the
first outdoor museums in the USA, and grew out of an
experiment in utopian communal living.

PAGE 3: nowhere but in New England do stunning fall colors
like this draw visitors from all over the world, every year.

PAGE 4: the bogs of Massachusetts are the world's biggest
cranberry producers. Farms like Cranberry World show
farming history back to pre-Pilgrim days.

focus on
NEW ENGLAND
• inspiring places, beautiful spaces •

INTRODUCTION

Six states, a city called Boston, and home of the original Yankees – that's New England. It can claim to be the first clearly-defined region of the United States, without which there might not be a United States. Tucked away in the northeast corner of the land, closest to the country that gave it its name, England, it was from New England that the earliest revolutionary talk came and where the first shot was fired in the American Revolution.

To look at some of these perfect pastoral landscapes today, New England hardly has the look of revolutionary fervor, although the area still has a reputation for political individuality. That applies to some states more than others, of the six that make up New England: Connecticut, Maine, Massachusetts, New Hampshire, Rhode Island and Vermont.

The region's largest center is Boston, always a maverick among American cities. It probably has more nicknames than any other city in the States, known among other things as The City on the Hill, The Athens of America, The Cradle of Liberty or just plain old Beantown, thanks to its history of baked bean production. It's also known as Puritan City, as its founders were Puritans, and throughout these pages the Puritan/English influence can clearly be seen. Place names like Plymouth and Truro – and even Boston itself – hark back to the land the Pilgrim fathers left in order to come to the New World and seek religious peace.

In so many ways New England is little changed since those days of the European settlers. The landscape was carved out 10,000 years ago when the last of the retreating glaciers left North America and Canada, leaving behind in New England a jagged coastline, rugged mountains, lakes and hills. Mankind has encroached in the last few hundred years, but the area's 70,000 square miles, and population of fewer than 14 million people, still leaves plenty of breathing space.

Mount Washington in New Hampshire's White Mountains is, at 6,288ft, New England's highest point, and has the dubious distinction of being the windiest place on earth, where the fastest winds have been recorded. The White Mountains cover about one-quarter of the state of New Hamphire, and part of Maine. The Appalachian Mountains also run through New England, taking with them the nation's longest waymarked footpath, the Appalachian Trail, which starts (or ends) in New England. Its beauty as it passes through regions like the Beartown State Forest is captured in these pages.

New England's beauty is not just in forests and mountain ranges, though, it can be seen in a single fall leaf. The area is renowned for having the most stunning displays of fall colors, whether it be in one of its state forests or in a small Boston park. But it is colorful in other ways too, from the crimson cranberries of the Massachusetts bogs to the golden maple syrup and the vivid orange pumpkins found all over. Food is an important feature here, especially seafood. Due to the ravages of those ancient glaciers, Maine has been left with about 5,000 miles more coastline than California. In those inlets and harbors, Maine lobsters and oysters grow in abundance, and while the fishing industry may have grown much more commercial, to feed the appetites of millions of Americans, there are still regular fishing communities to be found, where family boats with a small crew go out to haul in the bounty of the sea.

Lighthouses warn of the dangers and lobster pots hint at the rewards of this maritime life, and it's a heritage which lingers long. Boston's harbors are a link with the past, and the condos where boats line up outside show that the maritime memories remain. Indeed New England is a land where memories do remain, as the states are filled with buildings that keep the past alive. Some are museums, some are places of worship, and some continue to be family homes, often occupied by the same families that have lived in them for several generations.

In Boston the John Hancock Tower, New England's tallest building, reflects in its windows a 19th-century church. The city's 18th-century Faneuil Hall now rubs shoulders with 21st-century bars and clubs. Harvard University, founded in 1836 and the oldest higher learning institution in the USA, still produces the nation's top scholars and presidents, artists and lawyers. Its old buildings, caught in the light of these pages, still inspire those who aspire to achieve. Throughout the beautiful and rich agricultural lands of New England, there are plenty who think they already have the best that life has to offer, simply by living in one of these six states, in this corner of the USA.

The aptly-named Swift River races through the forests of the White Mountains in New Hampshire and thunders over the lip of the Sabbaday Falls, which is a popular local hiking spot.
Opposite: Newport's Marble House Mansion was built in 1892 for William K. Vanderbilt, and is styled after the Trianon buildings in the grounds of the Palace at Versailles.
Pages 6–7: many of New Hampshire's covered bridges, like this one over the Swift River, date back to the 19th century. Idyllic now as the fall colors start to dab the branches of the trees, these bridges must also withstand heavy winter snows and the raging torrents of spring.

Fishermen in Truro, which is the summer home of artist Edward Hopper, enjoy the last golden rays of the sun as it sinks over Provincetown at the very tip of Cape Cod.
Opposite: 'Old Ironsides' got her nickname because cannonballs could not pierce her tough oak sides. The USS Constitution was built in 1797 and is the oldest commissioned vessel in the US Navy. She is now moored and used as a museum in the Charleston Navy Yard in Boston.

The fertile New Hampshire countryside allows this Canterbury orchard to grow strawberries, blueberries, peaches and pumpkins, as well as seven different varieties of apple.
Opposite: Acorn Street, with its cobbles and shutters, is one of the prettiest streets in the desirable Beacon Hill district of Boston. It is as reserved and dignified as the old Bostonian families who live here.

Boston's 1877 Trinity Church is reflected in the John Hancock Tower. The Tower's designer, I.M. Pei, also created the glass pyramid outside the Louvre in Paris, and the Rock and Roll Hall of Fame in Cleveland.

Boston's Prudential Center Skywalk, 700-feet above the city streets, gives panoramic 360-degree views of the city, but only until 6pm. It stays open late on July 4th, for night-time panoramas.

The statue of John Harvard has stood outside University Hall in Harvard since 1884. Over the years visitors have rubbed smooth the left shoe, as they touch it for good luck.

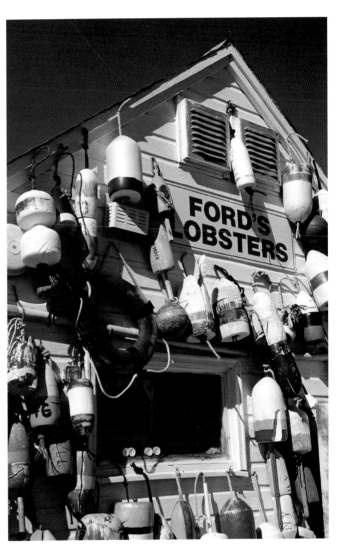

Ford's Lobsters is one of the most photographed buildings in little Noank, Connecticut, and appeared in the movie Mystic Pizza.

Before they had their own parish church, the people of Kennebunkport had to travel seven miles to Wells to go to church. The present building goes back to 1773, just in time to help them through the American Revolution. Opposite: the John Hancock Tower, the tallest building in New England, dwarfs much earlier office blocks in downtown Boston.

1775 lives again, as Concord people in period costume show how the American Revolution began here on the North Bridge in the Minute Man National Historical Park.
Opposite: a study in grace as an egret teaches her young to fish in the waters of a New Hampshire river.
Pages 20–21: since 1876 the light at the Nobska Lighthouse has flashed every six seconds to help mariners find their way along the coast of Cape Cod.

A rowing boat says 'Amen' to the beauty of Penobscot Bay, the deepest indentation on the Maine coastline where some of the last few traditional fishing villages still remain.

*At the dedication of King's Chapel in Boston in 1754, locals threw manure and dead animals in protest,
as they had thought that by coming to the New World they were escaping the Anglican Church.*

Edward Winslow, great-grandson of one of the Pilgrim Fathers who was also named Edward Winslow, built this house in Plymouth in 1754. Today it contains the Mayflower Society Museum. Opposite: Boston ancient and modern. Office blocks tower over the marketplace and, on the right, the 18th-century Faneuil Hall, surrounded now by bars, restaurants and nightcubs.

Boston's commercial heart beats across the harbor from Logan Airport. The growing airport handles more than 100,000 passengers every day.
Opposite: on the Waterfront in Boston's North End, where today's condos come, not with a car parking space or garage, but with a mooring for your boat.

These murals by John La Farge are among the features that resulted in Boston's Trinity Church being acclaimed as one of the Ten Most Significant Buildings in America.
Pages 30–31: no artist could create a palate of such bold yet subtle colors, as nature does every year in New England across every few inches of the leaf-carpeted ground.

Rocking chairs, pumpkins, a porch. The ideal spot from which to watch the golden leaves of fall.

At Mystic Seaport an historic seafaring town has been recreated, while the real Mystic maritime community still sits nearby at the outlet of Mystic River.

Opposite: Vermont's famous fall colors frame the campanile of Bennington's Old First Church. Completed in 1805, it was the first church in Vermont where church and state were separated, the state having no role in its administration.

Pages 34–35: water, water everywhere in Waterford, Connecticut, surrounding the town on three sides and creating a watery Eden for both young and old.

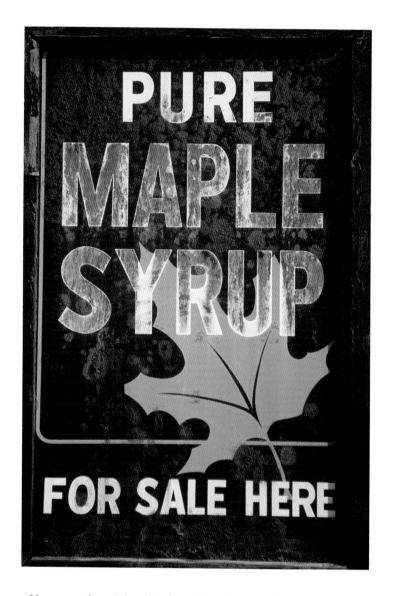

Vermont produces 2.3 million liters of maple syrup each year. That would
amount to four liters for every man, woman, and child in the state.
Opposite: a moment of reflection, in more ways than one, for these hikers
on a trail in the Beartown State Forest.
Pages 38–39: based at the Boston Fenway Park, the Red Sox are known
wherever baseball is played. At the back is the Green Monster Wall, the
highest in professional baseball.

Seafood in Maine is second to none, and though their oysters are not as well known as Maine lobsters, there are delicious specialties such as Eastern oysters and Cranberry Island oysters to be enjoyed.

As peaceful as the Italian cloister it resembles, this courtyard inside the Boston Public Library is one of the most peaceful spots in the city.

These colorful canoes are stacked outside an outlet for L.L.Bean in Freeport, Maine. Leon Leonwood Bean
started his business here, and the store on Main Street is now open 24/7.
Pages 44–45: just inside the main entrance to the Beartown State Forest, Benedict Pond covers 35 acres
and appeals to swimmers, fishermen, hikers, boaters, and anyone who loves nature.

Walking around Harvard is a history lesson in itself. Wadsworth House, built in 1726, is the university's second oldest building. It was built for the Harvard President, Benjamin Wadsworth, and was later to become General George Washington's HQ.

Boston's Freedom Trail is a 2.5-mile walk through the history of the city, easy to follow and impossible to forget.
Opposite: a pumpkin patch adds colorful fun to the history to be found in the Marsh-Billings National Historical Park
near Woodstock in Vermont, where the Billings Farm is both a historical site and a working farm.

'In grateful memory of the Harvard men who died in the World War, we have built this Church.' The Memorial Church in Harvard.
Opposite: you don't need to travel into New England to see the fabulous fall colors. Here in Boston's Arnold Arboretum at Harvard University there are golden tones in all their glory.
Pages 50–51: New England was the first area of the United States to be settled but the oldest residents are its tall, majestic trees, like these New Hampshire pines.

Independent Man looks down from the dome of the State Capitol in Providence, Rhode Island, standing atop one of the largest self-supporting domes in the world.

Opposite: from the 1,250-foot Mount Tom, the town of Woodstock shows why it was one of the first places in Vermont to be discovered by the outside world and turned into a fashionable place to escape.

At times New England's colors seem so rich as to be unreal, but these in the Beartown State Forest in the heart of the Berkshires are nature's natural palette.

Every journey begins with a single step. Kennebunkport's Seashore Trolley Museum began with a single trolley car in 1939 and it is now the largest collection of its kind in the world.

The fall colors aren't only up in the trees in Vermont, as these ripening pumpkins demonstrate.
Opposite: waves crash ashore on Mount Desert Island, much of which is given over to the Acadia National
Park. The national park has more than 47,000 acres of rugged coastline, granite mountains, woodland and
lakes on the Maine coast.
Pages 58–59: Newport at sunset. A restaurant deck and boats barely moving, the picture of serenity.
You can almost taste those Rhode Island blue crabs.

The Abenaki people gave Ogunquit its name which means 'the beautiful place by the sea'. This early
morning scene speaks for itself.
Opposite: known as Vermont's Little Grand Canyon, the 162-foot deep Quechee Gorge has at least
one advantage over its big brother – visitors can cross over it on footbridges.
Pages 62–63: the Shaker belief in simplicity is evident in the design of these buildings in the
19th-century Shaker village of Canterbury, where craftsmen still practice their traditional skills.

LOOKOUT TRAIL
TO VISTA

This Trail Is Open To:

CLOSED TO ALL
MOTORIZED VEHICLES

OFF-ROAD
VEHICLES
PROHIBITED
304 CMR 15.00

This modest entrance on the campus at Yale marks a repertory company that has won four Pulitzer Prizes, with many productions transferring to Broadway.
Opposite: The Beartown State Forest is one of eight national forests through which the Appalachian Trail passes.
Pages 66–67: pure waters, rocky shores and strong waves are what help give Maine lobsters their flavor. They don't come any fresher than straight off the boat.

2,175 miles, and a lot of signposts, mark the longest marked footpath in the United States.
It takes at least 5 million footsteps to hike all the way from Maine to Georgia.
Opposite: the golden leaves of these sugar maples plus the bright blue skies make for an
unbeatable color combination in New Hampshire's White Mountains.
Pages 70–71: whether these fishermen catch anything or not seems irrelevant, when the sunset
is as stunning as this at Race Point Beach in Provincetown.

Generations of Harvard students have been inspired simply by walking to class through the arched entrance of Sever Hall, completed in 1880. The name rhymes, appropriately, with 'clever'.
Pages 74–75: sand, dunes, rocks, water. Sachuest (or second) Beach at Middletown is one of Newport's most popular beaches because of its very simplicity.

The Massachusetts State House, where the state legislature meets, was built in 1798. Samuel Adams laid the cornerstone.

The peaceful wooden North Bridge in the Minute Man National Historical Park is where the first shot
was fired in the American Revolution, on April 19, 1775.
Pages 78–79: you can keep Manhattan. Sailboats on the Charles River on a sunny fall day, plus this
city skyline, are everything Bostonians want.

The original of Henry David Thoreau's simple one-room cabin stood by Walden Pond. 'If a man does not
keep pace with his companions, perhaps it is because he hears the beat of a different drummer.'

This 221-foot granite obelisk commemorates the 1775 Battle of Bunker Hill in Boston's Charlestown. The British won the battle but lost the war.
Opposite: the needle-like white steeple of this church in Stowe, Vermont has become a symbol of the town. The church is often photographed in winter snows too.

This coil of rope on the deck of a boat at Penobscot Bay in Maine is so simple and functional it could have come from the time when Henry Hudson sailed into the Bay in 1609.

Opposite: this roadside halt in Quechee, Vermont, has a real old-fashioned feel to it. Not as old as the famous Quechee Gorge though, which was formed more than 13,000 years ago.

Pages 84–85: the Wedding Cake House in Kennebunkport was much plainer when it was first put up by a shipbuilder in 1826. After a fire in 1852 he began adding the Gothic frosting, making it one of the most photographed buildings in Maine.

The Ivy League Brown University has been in Providence since 1770. Its 1904 Carrie Tower
is named after Caroline Mathilde Brown, who was the granddaughter of Nicholas Brown after
whom the university is named.
Opposite: the lighthouse tower overlooking South Beach at Chatham, on the east coast of Cape
Cod, was built in 1877 and is still an active coastguard station.

The Stars and Stripes flies proudly at Grafton's Old Tavern Inn. The inn, which was built in 1801, is still going strong. Guests have included Roosevelt, Rudyard Kipling, Ulysses S. Grant and Woodrow Wilson. Opposite: no matter which way the wind blows, the fishermen of Cape Cod must set out in their vessels. Visitors have the luxury of waiting for fair weather before setting out to sea on fishing trips.

Boston's Charles Street is noted for its antique shops, although if it's classic wines that you want then somewhere like this boutique wine store is the place to go.
Opposite: immortalized by Salem native Nathaniel Hawthorne in the book of the same name, the House of the Seven Gables was built in 1668 and is the oldest surviving wooden mansion in New England.
Pages 92–93: Boston's South End is one of the hippest parts of the city. Bistros and independent stores hide in among its impressive collection of Colonial-style houses.

INDEX

ACKNOWLEDGMENTS

The Automobile Association would like to thank the following photographers, companies and picture libraries for their assistance in the preparation of this book.

Abbreviations for the picture credits are as follows: - (t) top; (b) bottom; (l) left; (r) right; (AA) AA World Travel Library.
2t AA/M Lynch; 2c AA/C Sawyer; 2b AA/J Lynch; 3 AA/M Lynch; 4 AA/M Lynch; 6/7 AA/C Coe; 8 AA/C Coe; 9 AA/C Coe; 10 AA/M Lynch; 11 AA/C Coe; 12 AA/J Nicholson; 13 AA/M Lynch; 14 AA/C Sawyer; 15 AA/C Sawyer; 16/7 AA/C Coe; 17 AA/C Coe; 18 AA/C Coe; 19 AA/C Sawyer; 20/1 AA/J Lynch; 22 AA/J Lynch; 23 AA/M Lynch; 24 AA/M Lynch; 25 AA/C Sawyer; 26/7 AA/C Sawyer; 27 AA/M Lynch; 28 AA/C Sawyer; 29 AA/C Sawyer; 30/1 AA/M Lynch; 32 AA/C Sawyer; 33 AA/C Coe; 34/5 AA/M Lynch; 36 AA/M Lynch; 37 AA/M Lynch; 38/9 AA/J Nicholson; 40 AA/C Coe; 41 AA/C Coe; 42 AA/C Coe; 43 AA/C Sawyer; 44/5 AA/C Coe; 46 AA/M Lynch; 47 AA/J Nicholson; 48 AA/C Sawyer; 49 AA/J Nicholson; 50/1 AA/M Lynch; 52 AA/J Nicholson; 52/3 AA/C Saywer; 54 AA/C Coe; 55 AA/M Lynch; 56 AA/C Coe; 57 AA/M Lynch; 58/9 AA/M Lynch; 60 AA/M Lynch; 61 AA/M Lynch; 62/3 AA/M Lynch; 64 AA/M Lynch; 65 AA/C Coe; 66/7 AA/M Lynch; 68 AA/C Coe; 69 AA/M Lynch; 70/1 AA/C Coe; 72 AA/M Lynch; 73 AA/C Coe; 74/5 AA/C Coe; 76/7 AA/C Sawyer; 77 AA/J Nicholson; 78/9 AA/C Sawyer; 80 AA/C Sawyer; 81 AA/J Lynch; 82 AA/M Lynch; 83 AA/C Sawyer; 84/5 AA/C Coe; 86/7 AA/M Lynch; 87 AA/M Lynch; 88 AA/M Lynch; 89 AA/M Lynch; 90 AA/M Lynch; 91 AA/M Lynch; 92/3 AA/J Nicholson; 94 AA/C Sawyer; 95 AA/C Sawyer.

Every effort has been made to trace the copyright holders, and we apologise in advance for any accidental errors. We would be happy to apply the corrections in the following edition of this publication.